H(
Ho'

Prepare Mail Drops,
and Ship Packages
(A Yogi's® Book)

Jackie McDonnell

Second Edition
Copyright © February 2021 by Jackie McDonnell
All rights reserved

Published by: Yogi's Books LLC
                 98953 Sacatar Ranch Road
                 Inyokern, CA 93527

FOOD

PREPARING MAIL DROPS

SHIPPING PACKAGES

FOOD

You're going on a hike. You've researched gear, picked out the perfect shoes, tested your sleeping bag and shelter, decided to hike with (or without!) trekking poles. You've convinced your friends and family that you are not crazy, you will not be eaten by a bear, and you do not need to take a gun. Perfect. You're almost ready. But what about food?

One of the great pleasures of hiking is that you can eat anything you get your hands on, and you will still lose weight. But what exactly should you eat on trail to stay energized? And how do you get your food?

Don't stress. Choosing lightweight nutritious trail food, organizing mail drops, and shipping packages can be challenging, but with a little thought and planning it really is simple.

Let's get right to it!

HIKER HUNGER

Hiker hunger: The feeling of constant hunger accompanied by nonstop thoughts about food. Once hiker hunger hits, it stays with you for the duration of your hike (and sometimes for several weeks after finishing).

Long distance hikers are ALWAYS hungry, and every conversation eventually turns to feet, bowel movements, and food (not necessarily in that order!). While hiking, your mind will perpetually swirl around thoughts about food: What will I eat for my next snack? Should dinner be Ramen with tuna or Instant Refried Beans? Where will I eat when I get to town? How many snacks do I have left until I get to town? How long will my bag of Fritos last? Do I have enough Snickers bars?

But . . . . . hiker hunger does not start on day one. It usually takes about two weeks for hiker hunger to kick in, so plan accordingly. Once hiker hunger kicks in, you'll carry about 3000-4000 calories (~ 2 pounds) of food per day.

How do you feed your hiker hunger? First and foremost: <u>TASTE</u>. Taste is important. You must like your food! There's nothing worse than being out on the trail with a food bag full of stuff you hate. So try it before you hike with it! Prior to your hike, taste a variety of bars, trail mix, breakfasts, dinners, etc. Prepare the food exactly as you will on the trail. For example, many Knorr Pasta and Rice Sides call for butter and milk. On the trail you will not have butter and milk. You will prepare those dinners on trail with water alone, or perhaps with Butter Buds, powdered milk, and olive oil. Duplicate that process when trying out meals prior to your hike.

<u>VARIETY</u> is key, especially if your resupply strategy is primarily mail drops. Find at least 10-15 dinners, 30-ish snacks, and a few different lunch foods which you consider delicious. DEE-LISH-US ! ! ! Occasionally

include prepared meals as an extra treat (Good To-Go, Mountain House, AlpineAire, Peak Refuel, etc.).

Trail food should be QUICK AND EASY TO PREPARE. Long distance hikers do not cook. Instead, we boil water, add food, wait 10-15 minutes, EAT! This is completely different from actually cooking or preparing food. Do not choose dinners which call for a lengthy boil or simmer time. You will get frustrated waiting for your meal to be ready, plus you will use way too much fuel.

HINT: To save fuel, do not boil/simmer according to the directions. For example, the instructions on Knorr Pasta and Rice Sides direct users to simmer the pasta/rice for several minutes. Instead, for Pasta Sides: boil water, add the pasta/seasoning, stir, keep on stove for a minute or two longer, remove the pot from the stove, put lid on pot, place pot in pot cozy, wait 10-12 minutes, open lid. Dinner is ready! For Rice Sides, add the rice/seasoning to the water before turning on your stove, boil water/rice/seasoning mix, keep on stove for a minute or two after reaching a boil, remove the pot from the stove, put lid on pot, place pot in pot cozy, wait 10-12 minutes, open lid. Dinner is ready!

Hiker hunger also affects TOWN FOOD. You will be tempted to overload on restaurant food the second you hit town. Although you are extremely hungry, try to spread out your town food consumption. If you wolf down a gigantic burger, huge order of fries, and a large milkshake all at once, your body will not be able to absorb all the nutrients. You'll spend money on food which you will end up pooping out in a few hours.

Instead, eat the gigantic burger, then go get your motel room. Shower, do laundry, relax, then go back a few hours later for the fries and milkshake (eat, shower, eat again!).

The <u>FIRST DAY OUT OF TOWN</u> is a great opportunity to mix up your trail diet. Pack out pizza, deli sandwiches, Subway sandwiches, chips, Fritos, etc.

PACK LIGHT, EAT RIGHT

Hikers spend an incredible amount of time choosing the proper gear, but often put very little thought into trail food! The food you carry should matter. Choosing nutritional food contributes more to the enjoyment of a hike than shaving an extra six ounces off your pack weight. Carrying food which does not fuel your body efficiently is wasted weight.

There are many books and internet sites devoted to training and nutrition for endurance athletes (marathon runners, bicyclists, triathletes, etc.) who participate in sporting events which may last for an afternoon or a weekend. Conversely, a long distance hiker's endurance "event" lasts many weeks or months! Long distance hikers typically hike for 10-14 hours per day, 6-7 days a week, for many weeks or months straight — a marathon or close to it each and every day. The amount of energy required to keep your body going under these circumstances is unmatched in any other sport.

There simply wasn't any literature devoted specifically to the nutrition and training requirements of long distance hikers. Dr. Brenda Braaten changed all that! Brenda is a Registered Dietitian and holds a Ph.D. in Biochemical Nutrition from Tufts University. She has thru-hiked the Appalachian Trail and the Long Trail; she has climbed Mt. Shasta in California and all the 4000-foot peaks in the White Mountains of New England; she has backpacked in the Grand Canyon, Glacier National Park, Iceland, and New Zealand. In short, Brenda knows what she is talking about and has the hiking experience and education to back it up.

Brenda's sabbatical research into thru-hiker nutrition and training is presented in her article *"Pack Light, Eat Right – Nutritional recommendations for backpackers and other endurance exercise enthusiasts"*. In that article, Brenda states: "The body has a remarkable reserve capacity of nutrients, minerals and vitamins to buffer against short-term deficiencies or fluctuations in your diet. But long-term neglect will take a toll on your health, your performance, (and) your enjoyment of your wilderness experience. For backpackers, it is critical to consider how to optimize nutrient quality, while minimizing the weight/bulk of both the food and fuel carried."

It is highly recommended that you print *"Pack Light, Eat Right"*, then study it very carefully. Find yourself a quiet place where you can pore through Brenda's research.

The importance of proper nutrition cannot be stressed enough. It can make or break a hike. Fully understanding *"Pack Light, Eat Right"* is just as important as choosing the proper backpack, shoes, or shelter.

To read *"Pack Light, Eat Right"*, click the GEAR TALK tab at [www.triplecrownoutfitters.com].

NUTRIENTS

Early in my hiking career, I watched other hikers and soaked up as much knowledge I could. One thing I watched with fascination was the foods different hikers ate, followed by energy levels. I also paid attention to my own food intake and energy (or lack thereof). I knew I wasn't eating efficiently on trail, but I didn't know how to change or where to find quality trail food advice.

Luckily, during one of my early PCT hikes I had the good fortune to meet Dr. Brenda Braaten. Brenda and her husband, Laurie, operated a hiker hostel along the PCT for many years. When I stayed with the Braatens, I spoke with Brenda briefly about trail nutrition. The advice she gave me during that visit changed my energy level for the rest of that hike.

Before my next hike, I flew out to California and spent an entire afternoon picking Brenda's brain about trail nutrition. Brenda's nutrition advice improved my subsequent hikes tremendously! Her main suggestions were to graze throughout the day, increase my fat intake, dilute electrolyte drinks, and pay attention to my macronutrient mix.

Snack All Day

Brenda said something like, "Endurance athletes need to constantly fuel their bodies. That means snacking on carbs/fats at least every 75 minutes. And, yes, long distance hikers ARE endurance athletes!"

Prior to receiving this advice, my trail eating pattern was breakfast, snack, lunch, snack, dinner. I believe the major factor that increased my hiking energy level was this one simple change: removing lunch and instead snacking every 60-75 minutes.

Fats

Brenda also told me to make sure my trail diet is around 40% fats ("but that's your trail diet, Jackie. Do not eat like that at home!").

At home, you probably look at the "Nutrition Facts" labels to find foods with low fat content. When choosing hiking food, you'll do just the opposite: you want foods with high fat content. There are a couple major reasons for this:

- <u>Fat calories provide a longer burn</u>. The energy you get from fat calories stays with you longer, which is important for long distance hiking.

- <u>Fat has 252 calories per ounce</u>. Carbs and protein have 112 calories per ounce. You carry all your food. You'll get more calories per ounce from calorie-dense foods than from calorie-light foods. For example, see the comparison of tuna in water to tuna in sunflower oil on page 25.

Electrolytes

Electrolyte drinks are an important part of any hiking nutrition regimen. When you feel your energy dwindling, an electrolyte drink will boost your energy. However, electrolyte drinks like Gatorade, Propel, MiO, etc., are formulated for runners who need a quick boost of energy. Long distance athletes need a slower boost, so long distance hikers should dilute sports drinks. Add about 1/3 more water than the drink mix calls for.

Macronutrient Mix

Brenda recommends this trail diet:

> 45-55% Calories from carbohydrate
> 35-40% Calories from fat
> 10-15% Calories from protein

The above ratio applies to your overall trail diet; don't worry about hitting it on every individual food.

CHOOSING TRAIL FOOD

Enjoy Your Food

Whether you resupply using mail drops or buy food along the way, you need a basic understanding of what foods work for YOU. In other words, carry food that you like to eat. That may sound obvious, but you would be surprised at the number of hikers who send mail drop food which they don't like. For example, they read on someone's social media post that XYZ energy bar is fantastic. They try XYZ energy bar at home, it tastes okay, they think it is the be-all and end-all for their hike. They then fill all their mail drops with XYZ energy bars. When on trail, they quickly tire of XYZ energy bars. They pick up their mail drop, throw their mailed food right into the hiker swap boxes, then go to the local trail town store to buy food which appeals to them today. Don't be that hiker! It's a waste of money.

Before your hike, take time to try many different dinners, snacks, breakfasts, etc. Don't just try a food one time. Schedule a 3+ day period where you have time to hike 5+ miles a day for 3+ days. Eat only trail food, prepared exactly as you would prepare it on the trail. Although this does not exactly recreate a trail experience, it will give you a good idea of trail food specific to you. Get a feel for what you like and do not like. Then put together a selection of those foods while attempting to hit the macronutrient mix listed above.

Breakfast Ideas

Cereal with powdered milk, muesli, Pop-Tarts, granola bars, tortillas with peanut butter, dried fruit, granola, GORP, instant oatmeal, fresh fruit, nuts, berries, honey, hot Emergen-C, Carnation Breakfast Essentials, coffee, tea, hot chocolate (important for cold weather situations), vitamins.

Snack Ideas

Pretzels, Fritos, Snickers bars, granola bars, energy bars, protein bars, candy bars, chocolate, snack packet crackers, nuts, dried fruit, fresh fruit, jerky, GORP, trail mix, hard candy, cookies, fruit leathers, pre-cooked bacon, seaweed.

Lunch Ideas

Tortillas, bread, crackers, bagels, or pita bread combined with: peanut butter and jelly, Nutella, cheese and meat (pepperoni, salami, ham, roast beef), cream cheese, mustard, mayonnaise.

Dinner Ideas

Knorr Rice Sides, Knorr Pasta Sides, Pasta-Roni, instant mashed potatoes, Ramen, instant refried beans, stuffing, soups, cous-cous, quinoa, pasta/rice combined with flavor packets, prepared meals (Mountain House, AlpineAire, Peak Refuel, Good To-Go, etc.).

You could add: foil packet tuna/salmon/chicken, canned tuna/chicken, Spam, pepperoni, summer sausage, salami, crumbled bacon, TVP, Butter Buds, salt/pepper, spices, onions, garlic, shallots.

Idahoan brand mashed potatoes are a hiker staple. You might think that all brands of mashed potatoes are created equal. Oh, no! Not true! Other brands have the texture of clay. If you've got a choice, get the Idahoan. They come in packages like Knorrs; use one whole package for one meal.

Pasta Roni and Knorr Rice/Pasta Sides are hiker favorites because they are lightweight, inexpensive, available at even the smallest stores, and quick to prepare. Knorr Rice Sides have more calories per package than Knorr Pasta Sides. When choosing pasta meals, pay attention to the style of noodle. Angel hair noodles and flat noodles cook faster than shell, curly, or thicker noodles. Cooking faster = less fuel = lighter pack weight.

Small three ounce bags of real bacon pieces are found in the grocery store salad dressing section; bacon pieces are a great addition to any dinner.

Salt and pepper make all the difference in the world.

Butter Buds (powdered butter flavor) are found in the grocery store spice section.

Add olive oil to every dinner. One tablespoon gives you 120 calories. Olive oil has the best calorie-to-weight ratio of any trail food.

HOW MUCH TRAIL FOOD PER DAY?

Hikers do not all have the same hunger. There is a very good chance that the suggestions in this book will not exactly match your experience.

Some people have hiker hunger starting on the first day. Most people build up their hiker hunger over the first two weeks on trail. You certainly don't want to go hungry on trail, but you also don't want to carry unnecessary weight in the form of uneaten food. So what do you do? Select a wide variety of breakfast and dinner meals that you like. Then fill out the remainder of the day with snacks and perhaps a midday meal. Fewer/smaller snacks for the first two weeks, more snacks for the rest of the hike.

To keep your body properly fueled, try to eat a snack with carbs and fat every 60-75 minutes. At the beginning of the hike, those snacks will be smaller than they are after a couple weeks on trail. Determine how many hours you plan to hike each day, divide that into 60-75 minute sections, and plan one snack for each section. At the beginning of the hike, that snack may be half of a Clif Bar. Later in the hike, you will eat a whole bar for a snack.

If you like to take a long midday break, consider having a larger snack/lunch during that time. A long midday rest allows you to relax, refuel, and split the day into two parts. Some hikers cook a dinner during their midday break, making their evening meal more of a lunch.

Daily mileage and terrain will affect your food requirements. For example, if you are starting an

Appalachian Trail hike and plan to hike 10-15 miles per day, you will need less food than you would starting the Pacific Crest Trail or Continental Divide Trail where you plan to hike 20-25 miles per day.

At the beginning of your hike, pack about 2/3 of the calories you think you will need later in the hike. Over time, build up to about two pounds (3000-4000 calories) of food per day.

There isn't one correct way to break down hiker daily caloric intake. It's important to <u>carry nutritious food which you enjoy eating</u>. If everyone around you is eating Clif Bars but you hate Clif Bars, don't carry them! It's fun to talk about food with other hikers and to get new food ideas. But remember to do what works for you.

SHOPPING

Some hikers prepare/dehydrate their own personal favorite foods. Others purchase foods at their local supermarket, Walmart, Sam's Club, Costco, etc.

If you are resupplying primarily using mail drops, it makes sense to join Sam's Club and/or Costco. Snacks and bars are cheap at these discount stores, so you will most likely save more than the cost of the membership. Sam's Club has a much larger selection of bars and snacks than Costco. However, Costco has delicious, inexpensive Kirkland brand protein bars and nut bars (very similar to Kind bars).

But you can't find everything you want at Costco and Sam's Club. Next stop? Walmart and supermarkets! Walmart usually has inexpensive trail food. Chain supermarkets often have great deals on trail food in their weekly sales. Peruse the supermarket ads which show up in your mailbox each week. You can often find great weekly deals (cheaper than Walmart) in the chain supermarkets.

Grocery stores such as Sprouts and Whole Foods have bulk fruits, nuts, and trail mix. These offerings allow you to inject great variety into your trail diet. Unfortunately, bulk food goes stale or spoil very quickly. If you prepare all your mail drop food prior to your hike, bulk food might not be a good idea. However, if your home resupply person can pick up bulk food shortly before mailing, then this is a good option. Just be sure to use a Food Saver to vac-seal bulk food before shipping it to the hiker.

Do not open up granola or jerky bags and then split them into smaller portions for different mail drops. If you do, you will end up with rock-hard granola and jerky. When shipping mail drops, these foods are best left in their original packaging.

TRAIL FOOD EXAMPLES

The next section lists a Sample Five Day Resupply (see page 42) created using foods easily found at Walmart, supermarkets, Costco, and Sam's Club. Obviously, there are other food options as well as other places to shop (Trader Joe's, Whole Foods, Big Lots, etc.). This is simply an example.

To obtain the data for the Sample Five Day Resupply, we took nutrient information for several different foods, and for different flavors of the same foods. That data is shown in the following tables, which require a bit of explaining:

- <u>Calorie counts are not exact</u>, due to rounding.

- <u>Calorie and gram numbers are per package</u>, NOT per serving (unless indicated "per serving"). A trail meal is usually the whole package, so the calorie count per serving doesn't matter; the calorie count per package does matter.

- If a food label shows different calorie/gram numbers for "prepared" and "mix/package," <u>this book uses the "mix/package" numbers</u>. For example, Knorr Pasta Side "prepared" data often assumes you are adding butter and milk. Chances are *really* good that you will not have butter and milk with you on trail. So, our data uses the "mix/package" information.

- <u>Some tables finish with an "average" row</u>. This is helpful when choosing a food which has many different flavor variations. Continuing with our Knorr

Pasta Side example: Knorr has many Pasta Side flavor options. We included seven on our table (below). We then averaged the nutrient information for those seven flavors. Using an average allows us to simply list "Knorr Pasta" in the Sample Five Day Resupply list without specifying a flavor.

Knorr Pasta Sides	Weight		Calories			
	g	oz	Total	Fat	Carbs	Protein
Teriyaki Noodles	130	4.6	548	40	445	64
Creamy Garlic Shells	124	4.4	470	18	390	62
Parmesan	121	4.3	472	70	330	72
Cheesy Spinach Dip	116	4.1	462	50	339	73
Cheddar Broccoli	121	4.3	460	40	357	63
Four Cheese	116	4.1	450	36	351	63
Stroganoff	113	4.0	420	27	333	60
AVERAGE	120	4.3	469	40	364	65

Knorr Rice Sides	Weight		Calories			
	g	oz	Total	Fat	Carbs	Protein
Teriyaki Rice	153	5.4	645	37	547	61
Herb & Butter	153	5.4	575	10	497	68
Red Beans & Rice	144	5.1	585	25	487	73
Cheddar Broccoli	161	5.7	573	37	467	70
Spanish	158	5.6	552	25	468	60
Taco	153	5.4	542	25	458	60
Chicken	158	5.6	600	45	488	67
AVERAGE	154	5.5	582	29	487	66

Zatarain's Rice	Weight		Calories			
	g	oz	Total	Fat	Carbs	Protein
Dirty Rice (GF)	226	8	780	30	677	73
Jambalaya (GF)	226	8	800	25	691	84
Cilantro Lime (GF)	195	6.9	700	35	610	55
Yellow Rice (GF)	195	6.9	700	17	624	58
Red Beans & Rice	226	8	805	17	659	129
Spanish	195	6.9	720	22	622	75
Cheddar Broccoli	161	5.7	600	62	458	80
AVERAGE	203	7.2	729	30	620	79

Knorr Rice Sides contain pasta, therefore are not gluten-free. Zatarain's Rice has several gluten-free flavors (not flavors all are gluten-free). One package of Zatarain's Rice is much larger than one Knorr Rice Side. You can split one Zatarain's into two meals using ziplock bags.

Mexicali Rose Instant Refried Beans	Weight		Calories			
	g	oz	Total	Fat	Carbs	Protein
Homestyle	170	6	635	104	415	116
Fat Free	170	6	600	0	456	144
AVERAGE	170	6	618	52	436	130

Santa Fe Instant Refried Beans	Weight		Calories			
	g	oz	Total	Fat	Carbs	Protein
Fat Free Black	205	7.25	780	0	612	168
Fat Free Vegetarian	205	7.25	768	0	594	174
Southwestern	205	7.25	780	108	512	160
AVERAGE	205	7	776	36	573	167

Instant Refried Beans are quick to prepare, extremely filling, and delicious. They can be eaten plain, on a tortilla, scooped up with Fritos, etc.

Maruchan Ramen 85 g 3 oz	Calories			
	Total	Fat	Carbs	Protein
Chicken Flavor	380	140	208	32
Beef Flavor	380	140	208	32
Shrimp Flavor	380	140	208	32
Chili Flavor	380	140	201	39
Soy Sauce Flavor	380	140	201	39
Pork Flavor	380	140	200	40
AVERAGE	380	140	204	36

Top Ramen 85 g 3 oz	Calories			
	Total	Fat	Carbs	Protein
Chicken Flavor	380	120	218	42
Beef Flavor	380	120	225	35
Shrimp Flavor	380	120	225	35
Chili Flavor (Vegetarian)	380	120	225	35
Soy Sauce Flavor (Vegetarian)	380	120	219	41
Hot & Spicy Beef Flavor	380	120	219	41
AVERAGE	380	120	222	38

Ramen is loaded with fat, inexpensive, and cooks quickly. Many hikers add a package of Ramen to a Knorr Side. Mix in tuna/salmon/chicken/Spam for flavor and protein.

StarKist Tuna and Salmon Creations 74 g 2.6 oz	Total Cal	Fat Cal	Carbs Cal	Protein	
				Cal	g
Tuna - Lemon Pepper	80	5	3	72	18
Tuna - Sweet & Spicy	90	5	17	68	18
Tuna - Hickory Smoked	110	30	0	80	20
Tuna - Herb & Garlic	110	35	11	64	16
Tuna - Ranch	80	20	4	56	14
Tuna - Hot Buffalo	70	5	0	65	16
Salmon - Lemon Dill	90	25	6	59	14
AVERAGE	90	17	6	68	17

StarKist Chicken Creations 74 g 2.6 oz	Total Cal	Fat Cal	Carbs Cal	Protein	
				Cal	g
Chicken Salad	70	18	16	36	9
Zesty Lemon Pepper	70	18	16	36	9
Buffalo Style	80	27	17	36	9
Ginger Soy	90	27	23	40	10
AVERAGE	78	23	18	37	9

Tuna, Salmon, and Chicken Creations add flavor, texture, and protein to Ramen, Knorr Sides, and Idahoan mashed potatoes.

StarKist Tuna or Salmon	Weight		Total Cal	Fat Cal	Carbs Cal	Protein	
	g	oz				Cal	g
Tuna Salad	85	3	100	30	14	56	14
Chunk Light Tuna in Sunflower Oil	74	2.6	150	81	0	69	17
Chunk Light Tuna in Water	74	2.6	70	5	0	65	17
Pink Salmon in Water	74	2.6	70	10	2	58	15
Salmon Creations, Lemon Dill	74	2.6	90	25	6	59	14

Tuna and salmon come in both cans and foil packets. Foil packets are best for trail food.

Adding tuna or salmon to an evening meal is a great way to add flavor, texture, and protein.

Notice the difference in fat calories in Tuna in Sunflower Oil compared to Tuna Creations, Tuna in Water, or Salmon. They all weigh 2.6 ounces, yet Tuna/Chicken Creations have an average of 90 calories, Tuna/Salmon in Water have 70 calories, and Tuna in Sunflower Oil has 150 calories. Remember, fat calories are the hiker's friend!

Meats	Weight		Total Cal	Fat Cal	Carbs Cal	Protein	
	g	oz				Cal	g
Jack Link's Original Jerky	92	3.25	240	30	78	132	33
Jack Link's Peppered Jerky	92	3.25	240	15	105	120	10
Jack Link's Teriyaki Jerky	92	3.25	240	30	78	132	33
Pacific Gold Original Jerky	35	1	90	10	28	52	13
Tyson Premium White Chicken	198	7	245	53	0	192	49
Tyson Premium Grilled Chunk White Chicken	198	7	245	53	0	192	46
Spam Single Classic	71	2.5	210	160	14	36	9
Bridgford Summer Sausage	448	16	1520	1200	0	320	36
Bridgford Pepperoni Stick	448	16	1760	1760	0	320	96
Hormel Pepperoni Slices	170	6	900	780	0	120	30

Meats details above are per package, not per serving, due to the fact that hikers typically do not split products into smaller servings. For example, you will carry the entire 16 ounce summer sausage and consume it over your five day resupply section.

Trail Mix	Weight		Calories			
	g	oz	Total	Fat	Carbs	Protein
Kirkland Signature	57	2	300	160	104	36
Kar's Sweet & Salty	57	2	270	162	76	32
Kar's Sweet & Salty	99	3.5	490	283	151	56
Kar's All Energy	85	3	420	243	133	44
Kar's Raisin Almond Cashew	78	2.75	320	144	144	32
AVERAGE	75	2.65	360	198	122	40

Orchard Valley Harvest Trail Mix	Weight		Calories			
	g	oz	Total	Fat	Carbs	Protein
Cranberry, Almond, Cashew	52	1.9	250	150	76	24
Antioxidant Mix	56	2	270	150	96	24
Omega-3 Mix	56	2	290	200	62	28
Heart Healthy Blend	56	2	290	180	82	28
Chocolate Raisin Nut	56	2	290	200	58	32
Cherries & Dark Choc	53	1.9	230	120	98	12
Almonds & Dark Choc	56	2	300	220	56	24
Blueberries & Dk Choc	53	1.9	240	130	98	12
AVERAGE	55	2	270	169	78	23

Trail mix is high in fat and has a great calorie-to-weight ratio, so it's a good snack to carry. Hikers typically tire of trail mix early in the hike. To avoid trail mix burnout, include many different trail mix varieties in your trail diet.

Candy	Weight		Calories			
	g	oz	Total	Fat	Carbs	Protein
Baby Ruth	54	1.9	260	108	140	12
Snickers	52	1.86	250	110	124	16
M&M's Peanut	49	1.74	250	120	110	20
Butterfinger	54	1.9	250	90	148	12
Twix	51	1.79	250	108	136	8
Payday	52	1.85	240	117	95	28
Nestle Crunch	44	1.55	230	108	114	8
M&M's Plain	47	1.69	230	80	142	8
Almond Joy	45	1.61	220	117	95	8
Hershey's Milk Chocolate	43	1.55	220	117	91	12
Hershey's Milk Chocolate with Almonds	41	1.45	210	126	68	16
Reese's Take 5	42	1.5	210	99	99	12
Kit Kat	42	1.5	210	99	103	8
Heath	39	1.4	210	110	96	4
100 Grand	43	1.5	200	72	124	4
AVERAGE	74	2.6	366	170	175	21

Nature Valley Crunchy Bars 42 g 1.5 oz	Calories per package			
	Total	Fat	Carbs	Protein
Crunchy Oats 'n Honey	190	60	118	12
Crunchy Maple Brown Sugar	190	60	118	12
Crunchy Peanut Butter	190	80	96	14
AVERAGE	190	67	111	13

Nature Valley Fruit & Nut Bars 35 g 1.2 oz	Calories			
	Total	Fat	Carbs	Protein
Trail Mix	140	35	94	11
Dark Chocolate & Nut	140	35	97	8
Dark Chocolate Cherry	140	35	97	8
AVERAGE	140	35	96	9

Nature Valley Sweet & Salty Nut Bars 35 g 1.2 oz	Calories			
	Total	Fat	Carbs	Protein
Almond	160	60	88	12
Dk Choc, Peanut, Almond	160	70	79	11
Peanut	170	80	75	15
AVERAGE	163	70	81	13

Nature Valley bars come in many flavors and styles. They are inexpensive and found in even the smallest stores.

| Lara Bars (Gluten Free) | Calories | | | |
45 g 1.6 oz	Total	Fat	Carbs	Protein
Banana Chocolate Chip	190	44	127	19
Blueberry Muffin	190	44	131	15
Carrot Cake	190	41	134	15
Lemon Bar	200	53	126	21
Peanut Butter Chocolate Chip	210	63	121	26
Apple Pie	200	47	132	21
Cinnamon Roll	200	53	126	21
AVERAGE	197	49	128	20

| Luna Bars (Gluten Free) | Calories | | | |
48 g 1.69 oz	Total	Fat	Carbs	Protein
Sea Salt Caramel	190	60	98	32
Creamy Dreamy Peanut Butter	210	90	88	32
Lemon Zest	190	60	98	32
Nutz Over Chocolate	200	70	98	32
White Chocolate Macadamia	200	70	98	32
S'mores	190	60	98	32
Caramel Walnut Brownie	200	70	98	32
AVERAGE	197	69	97	32

Lara Bars typically have fewer than 6 simple ingredients which are actual food!   Luna Bars offer delicious flavor options.

ProBar 85 g 3 oz	Calories			
	Total	Fat	Carbs	Protein
Almond Cashew Crunch	390	162	192	36
Banana Nut Bread	400	180	184	36
Blueberry Muffin	400	189	171	40
Chocolate Coconut	390	162	196	32
Mocha Almond Fudge	370	153	177	40
Oatmeal Chocolate Chip	410	198	176	36
Original Trail Mix	370	153	181	36
Peanut Butter	390	189	153	48
Peanut Butter Choc Chip	400	198	158	44
S'Mores	400	189	171	40
Superberry and Greens	370	144	190	36
Superfood Slam	380	162	178	40
Superfruit Slam	370	135	203	32
Wholeberry Blast	370	144	194	32
AVERAGE	386	168	180	38

Meal replacement bars such as Greenbelly Meal2Go and ProBar provide a full meal without cooking. These are popular with longer resupply stretches and for hikers who cold soak.

Greenbelly Meal2Go and ProBars are available online.

Greenbelly Meal2Go 155 g 5.47 oz	Calories			
	Total	Fat	Carbs	Protein
Peanut Apricot	665	207	386	72
Dark Chocolate Banana	660	234	358	68
Cranberry Almond	650	216	366	68
Mango Cashew Coconut	665	225	376	64
Spiced Caramel Apple	695	261	362	72
AVERAGE	667	229	370	69

Clif Bars 68 g 2.4 oz	Calories			
	Total	Fat	Carbs	Protein
Blueberry Crisp	250	45	170	35
Peanut Butter Banana	260	70	153	37
Peanut Toffee Buzz	250	60	153	37
Cool Mint Chocolate	250	45	167	38
Chocolate Brownie	250	50	166	34
White Chocolate Macadamia Nut	260	70	156	34
Carrot Cake	250	40	175	35
AVERAGE	253	54	163	36

Clif Builder's Protein Bars 68 g 2.4 oz	Total Cal	Fat Cal	Carbs Cal	Protein	
				Cal	g
Chocolate Peanut Butter	280	90	110	80	20
Chocolate Mint	270	80	110	80	20
Vanilla Almond	270	80	110	80	20
Chocolate	270	80	110	80	20
Cinnamon Nut Swirl	270	80	110	80	20
Crunchy Peanut Butter	270	90	100	80	20
Cookies N Cream	260	70	110	80	20
AVERAGE	270	81	109	80	20

Luna Protein Bars (Gluten Free) 45 g 1.69 oz	Total Cal	Fat Cal	Carbs Cal	Protein	
				Cal	g
Chocolate Chip Cookie Dough	180	50	82	48	12
Chocolate Salted Caramel	180	45	87	48	12
Chocolate Peanut Butter	190	70	72	48	12
Mint Chocolate Chip	170	45	77	48	12
Berry Greek Yogurt	180	45	87	48	13
Chocolate Walnut Fudge	180	60	72	48	12
AVERAGE	180	53	80	48	12

RX Bars 52 g 1.83 oz	Total Cal	Fat Cal	Carbs Cal	Protein	
				Cal	g
Chocolate Sea Salt	210	81	81	48	12
Peanut Butter Chocolate	210	90	72	48	12
Blueberry	210	63	99	48	12
Peanut Butter	210	72	90	48	12
Coconut Chocolate	210	81	81	48	12
Mixed Berry	210	63	99	48	12
Mint Chocolate	210	81	81	48	12
AVERAGE	210	76	86	48	12

Premier Protein Bars 72 g 2.53 oz	Total Cal	Fat Cal	Carbs Cal	Protein	
				Cal	g
Chocolate Peanut Butter	290	70	100	120	30
Peanut Butter Crunch	300	90	90	120	30
Dark Chocolate Mint	280	60	100	120	30
Salted Caramel	290	60	110	120	30
Dark Chocolate Almond	290	70	100	120	30
Double Chocolate Crunch	270	60	90	120	30
Yogurt Peanut Crunch	290	70	100	120	30
AVERAGE	287	69	99	120	30

Protein Bars: RX Bars have simple ingredients (for example, egg whites, almonds, cashews, dates). Other protein bars have a long list of ingredients.

Pure Protein Bars (Gluten Free) 50 g 1.76 oz	Total Cal	Fat Cal	Carbs Cal	Protein	
				Cal	g
Chocolate Peanut Caramel	190	50	60	80	20
Chocolate Salted Caramel	200	45	79	76	19
Birthday Cake	200	45	75	80	20
Strawberry Greek Yogurt	190	40	70	80	20
Maple Caramel	190	50	64	76	19
Chocolate Deluxe	180	40	56	84	21
Chocolate Peanut Butter	200	50	70	80	20
AVERAGE	193	46	68	79	20

Kirkland Protein Bars 60 g 2.12 oz	Total Cal	Fat Cal	Carbs Cal	Protein	
				Cal	g
Chocolate Brownie	190	60	46	84	21
Chocolate Chip Cookie Dough	190	60	46	84	21
Cookies and Cream	190	50	52	88	22
Chocolate Peanut Butter Chunk	190	60	46	84	21
Cinnamon Roll	180	50	46	84	21
AVERAGE	188	56	47	85	21

Nature Valley Protein Bars 40 g 1.42 oz	Total Cal	Fat Cal	Carbs Cal	Protein	
				Cal	g
Peanut, Almond, & Dark Chocolate	190	110	40	40	10
Peanut Butter & Dark Chocolate	190	110	40	40	10
Salted Caramel Nut	190	100	50	40	10
AVERAGE	190	107	43	40	10

Lenny and Larry's Complete Cookie 114 g 4 oz	Total Cal	Fat Cal	Carbs Cal	Protein	
				Cal	g
Double Chocolate	400	140	196	64	16
Chocolate Chip	400	140	196	64	16
Birthday Cake	400	90	246	64	16
Lemon Poppy Seed	400	120	216	64	16
Snickerdoodle	400	120	216	64	16
White Chocolate Macadamia	420	120	236	64	16
Peanut Butter Chocolate Chip	440	200	176	64	16
AVERAGE	409	133	212	64	16

Condiments	Weight		Calories			
	g	oz	Total	Fat	Carbs	Protein
Nutella	371	13	1950	990	880	80
Jif Extra Crunchy	454	16	2660	1820	448	392
Jif Creamy	454	16	2660	1820	448	392
Skippy Super Chunk	462	16.3	2660	1960	308	392
Skippy Creamy	462	16.3	2660	1960	308	392
Great Value Creamy Stripes PB & Grape Jelly	510	18	2100	900	1000	200
Best Foods Mayonnaise	154	5.5	1100	1100	0	0
GEM Olive Oil (per bottle)	238	8.5	2040	2040	0	0
GEM Olive Oil (per tablespoon)	14	0.5	120	120	0	0
Biscoff Cookie Butter	400	14	2210	1287	871	52

Olive oil is the best calorie-to-weight ratio of all foods. Add it to every trail dinner.

Other condiments are great options for adding fat to your trail diet.

Cookie butter is freaking delicious.

Breads	Weight		Calories			
	g	oz	Total	Fat	Carbs	Protein
Mission Tortillas Soft Taco (10-pack)	496	17.5	1400	250	990	160
Mission Tortillas Soft Taco (per tortilla)	50	1.75	140	25	99	16
Sara Lee Plain Bagel, 6-pack	567	20	1560	108	1260	192
Nature's Own Honey Wheat Bread	567	20	1540	110	1166	264

Tortillas are great for trail sandwiches. Add peanut butter, honey, tuna, M&M's, instant refried beans, lunch meat and cheese, etc.

Bagels are a nice change of pace, but they take up a lot of pack space.

Use a loaf of bread to make peanut butter sandwiches or mayonnaise sandwiches, squish down the loaf, pack that out.

Quaker Instant Oatmeal (per individual packet)	Weight		Calories			
	g	oz	Total	Fat	Carbs	Protein
Maple & Brown Sugar	43	1.51	160	18	126	16
Cinnamon & Spice	43	1.51	160	18	126	16
Apples & Cinnamon	43	1.51	160	18	126	16
Strawberries & Cream	35	1.23	130	20	98	12
Blueberries & Cream	35	1.23	130	20	98	12
Peaches & Cream	35	1.23	130	25	93	12
Bananas & Cream	35	1.23	130	25	93	12
AVERAGE	38	1.4	143	21	109	14

<u>Oatmeal</u> is a quick, easy, filling trail breakfast. Most hikers use 2-3 packets per breakfast. Be sure to get instant oatmeal. Cooking regular oatmeal uses too much fuel.

Granola (per whole package)	Weight		Calories			
	g	oz	Total	Fat	Carbs	Protein
Honey Bunches of Oats Honey Roasted	311	11	1320	360	864	96
Nature Valley Oats 'n Honey	311	11	1260	300	720	240
Bear Naked Triple Berry	340	12	1320	165	1022	132
Sam's Choice Vanilla Almond Granola Clusters	311	11	1440	480	816	144
Clif Banana Nut Crunch	283	10	1300	360	780	160
Clif Blueberry Crisp	283	10	1250	360	730	160
Clif Cinnamon Almond Crunch	283	10	1300	360	780	160
Clif White Chocolate Macadamia Crunch	283	10	1250	360	730	160

Granola with powdered milk is a great breakfast cereal.

Granola isn't just for breakfast. You could make your own trail mix using granola, M&M's, and nuts.

Breakfast Drinks	Weight		Calories			
	g	oz	Total	Fat	Carbs	Protein
Nido (per container)	360	12.6	1920	960	624	336
Nido (per serving)	30	1	160	80	52	28
Great Value Instant Milk (per envelope)	91	3.2	320	0	192	128
Great Value Instant Milk (per serving)	23	.82	80	0	48	32
Carnation Instant Milk (per container)	272	8	960	0	576	384
Carnation Instant Milk (per serving)	23	0.82	80	0	48	32
Carnation Breakfast Essentials, per envelope: Classic French Vanilla, Rich Milk Choc, or Strawberry Sensation	36	1.26	130	0	110	20

Nido Dry Whole Milk is found in the grocery store Hispanic foods section.

Carnation Instant Milk and Great Value Instant Milk (both fat free) are found in the grocery store baking section.

Carnation Breakfast Essentials are great as a stand-alone drink and also added to a granola cereal, found in the grocery store cereal aisle.

SAMPLE FIVE DAY RESUPPLY

A five day resupply includes four breakfasts, four dinners, and five days' worth of snacks/lunch. You will eat breakfast in town on the first day of the resupply section, so you will not need a trail breakfast on Day 1. You will eat dinner in town on the last day of the resupply section, so you will not need a trail dinner on Day 5. Obviously, this assumes you leave the first town on day one in the morning and arrive in the second town on day five in the late afternoon. That will not always be the way your schedule works out.

The following "Sample Five Day Resupply" is for a hiker at least two weeks after the start of the hike who is hiking 10-14 hours per day. Hikers typically are not as hungry at the beginning of the hike. So, in the first few weeks of the hike, cut the tortillas and peanut butter in half, and delete about half of the snacks.

Days on trail	5	
Total calories	18,762	
Calories per day	3,752	Excluding one town breakfast and one town dinner
Pounds per day	1.91	
Snacks per day	8	plus lunch: tortillas/PB
Dinner	4	
Breakfast	4	

Sample Five Day Resupply	Weight		Calories			
	g	oz	Total	Fat	Carb	Protein
Breakfast						
Quaker Oatmeal (4) (2 per breakfast)	76	2.8	572	84	432	56
Carnation Breakfast Essentials (2)	72	2.5	260	0	220	40
NV Crunchy Bars (2)	84	3	380	134	222	26
Note: one breakfast = one Carn. Essentials + one NV bar one breakfast = two Quaker Oatmeal packets						
Dinner						
Knorr Rice Side	153	5.4	578	34	480	64
Knorr Pasta Side	120	4.3	470	44	359	67
Mexicali Rose Refried Beans Homestyle	170	6.0	600	104	415	116
Top Ramen	85	3.0	380	120	222	38
StarKist Tuna Creations	74	2.6	90	16	6	68
Spam Single	71	2.5	210	160	14	36
StarKist Chunk Light Tuna in Sunflower Oil	74	2.6	150	81	0	69
StarKist Pink Salmon	74	2.6	70	10	2	58
Gem Olive Oil (1 tbsp each dinner)	56	2.0	480	480	0	0

Sample Five Day Resupply	Weight		Calories			
	g	oz	Total	Fat	Carb	Protein
Snacks / Lunch						
Candy (5)	370	13	1830	850	875	105
Orchard Valley Harvest Trail Mix (5)	275	10	1350	845	390	115
Snickers (5)	52	1.86	1250	550	620	80
Lara Bars (5)	225	8	985	245	640	100
NV Protein Bars (5)	231	8.1	1330	980	154	196
Complete Cookie (3)	570	20	2045	665	1060	320
ProBars (2)	170	6	772	336	360	76
Clif Bars (5)	340	12	1265	270	815	180
Pure Protein Bars (5)	250	8.8	965	230	340	395
Tortillas (pack of 10)	496	18	1400	250	990	160
Skippy Super Chunk (1/2 jar)	231	8.1	1330	980	154	196
Total	4319	153	18762	7468	8770	2561
% of Total			100%	40%	47%	13%

PREPARING MAIL DROPS

RESUPPLY STRATEGY

Now that you know what you will eat on trail, you have to figure out how to get your food. There are three broad schools of thought concerning resupply:

- Mail all your food
- Buy all your food in trail towns
- Hybrid – a combination of mailing and buying in town

Mail Drops

What is a mail drop? It's a mailed box of food and/or gear which the hiker picks up during their hike. The mail drop can be shipped to a trail town Post Office, local business, motel, or person who is willing to accept hiker mail.

Hikers often make the mistake of preparing food mail drops for the duration of the hike. Although cherry pie Lara Bars or bacon mac-and-cheese seem tasty today, you might sing a different tune after eating the same foods every single week. A mail drop resupply strategy is only recommended for hikers who have dietary restrictions or who are 100% sure they will not tire of their mail drop food.

Mail Drop Strategy Pros

- <u>Food selection</u>. Resupply locations which are primarily convenience stores and resorts often have limited food selection. Sending a mail drop to such a location allows you to eat the food you like.

- <u>Speed</u>. Jet into town, pick up your mail drop, then quickly return to the trail.

- <u>Time to relax</u>. Pick up your mail drop, get a motel room, then relax with your feet up rather than spending time on your feet shopping.

Mail Drop Strategy Cons

- <u>You have no idea how much you are going to eat</u>. You will eat A LOT. What you think will be enough food as you sit at home right now will not be enough. You'll end up supplementing your mail drop with food bought in trail towns. Why not just buy ALL your food there and save the postage?

- <u>You'll get sick of your mail drop food</u>. Suppose you send yourself this mail drop (which is too small). It's July. You prepared the package in April. You've been eating the same food for three months. You now hate the food in your packages. You pick up your mail drop and throw all the food you hate into the hiker swap box, then go to the local store to buy food which appeals to you TODAY. You've paid for food you didn't want (plus postage). And, look at this, you're at the store in town, where you could have just bought all your food to begin with.

- <u>Postage is expensive</u>. If shipping using USPS, ALWAYS choose Priority Mail. If you have any desire to actually receive your package, never, ever, ever ship your package using a less expensive USPS option (exception: packages containing fuel, see page 62). USPS Priority Mail, UPS, and FedEx are all very expensive. If you buy in town, you don't pay postage.

- <u>You'll be tied to a schedule</u>. Post Offices have limited hours of operation. You'll constantly alter your hike to make it to town when the Post Office is open. For example, instead of relaxing by a lake with your hiking buddies, you need to keep moving to make it to town for the PO.

If the PO closes at 2pm on Friday and you arrive at 3pm on Friday, you will wait in town until Monday morning. That's three days spending money on motel rooms and restaurant food.

Buy in Trail Towns

If the resupply locations for your hike are primarily supermarkets and grocery stores, it makes sense to buy in town. You'll have the same selection at a supermarket in a trail town as you would have at a supermarket near your home.

Buy in town pros

- Not tied to a schedule. Supermarkets are open every day, usually 24 hours a day or from 6am-11pm. It doesn't matter when you get to town, you can always resupply.

- Variety. You can change up your trail diet on the fly. Sick of ramen and tuna? Buy something different.

- Save on postage. How many times will you resupply on a 5 month hike? 25 times? In 2021, the cost to ship a USPS Large Flat Rate box is $21.90. You can save $547.50 if you resupply in town ($21.90 x 25 = $547.50).

- Support local economy. It's good PR for the trail and for hikers if you support businesses along the trail.

Buy in town cons

- <u>Time spent shopping</u>. Instead of relaxing in your motel room, you'll be at the supermarket, on your feet.

- <u>Lack of favorite foods</u>. Local stores might not have your favorite flavor of popular foods. For example, if you *really* like Picante Beef Ramen, you probably won't find that in a local supermarket.

Hybrid Resupply

Using a hybrid resupply strategy, you'll buy food at most locations, and pick up resupply packages at places where there is inadequate food available (i.e. resorts or towns that only have convenience stores). Consult the guidebook for your trail to find out which locations are suitable for a mail drop and which locations have a supermarket or grocery store.

You do not need to have a home resupply person ship packages to you. If you know that a location farther up the trail requires a mail drop, simply prepare that mail drop from a previous town. Ship the package to yourself farther up the trail.

If you don't want to go to the trouble to purchase food, prepare the package, and find the trail town Post Office, an alternative is to use a <u>trail resupply company</u>

such as Zero Day Resupply [www.zerodayresupply.com]. Zero Day Resupply is owned/operated by Chris Solinsky, a Triple Crown Hiker (meaning he has thru-hiked the Appalachian Trail, Pacific Crest Trail, and Continental Divide Trail). Because Chris is a hiker, he knows the importance of food variety and of receiving resupply packages on time. Zero Day Resupply has an extensive food selection, and their phone app is built specifically to operate when cell service is weak. You can literally do your shopping anyplace you have cell service, including on the trail. When you get to town, your resupply package is waiting for you. Pick up the package, then RELAX.

POSTAGE COST

Depending upon the distance from your home to your trail, it could be cost effective or very expensive to resupply using mail drops. For example, if you live in California and you are planning an Appalachian Trail hike, mail drop postage will be very expensive. Postage cost will be $15.50+ for every mail drop. However, if you live in California and you are planning a Pacific Crest Trail hike, postage for each mail drop could cost as little as $7.83 (see page 74).

PACKING RESUPPLY BOXES

Food, fuel, maps, shoes, clothing, how do you pack it all?

- Determine the <u>cheapest trackable shipping method</u>, which is usually USPS Priority Mail. Use the shipping estimate tools on the USPS, UPS, and FedEx websites.

  USPS Priority Mail: Regional Rate boxes are good for shorter shipping distances, Flat Rate boxes are good for longer distances. The differences are discussed in the Priority Mail section, beginning on page 69.

- With careful packing, you can fit <u>four days of food into a USPS Priority Mail Regional Rate Box A1</u>.

  ‣ Line up all your bars in the box like pencils in a cup.

  ‣ Poke a tiny hole in any food package that is filled with air (i.e. pasta, rice, potato, and instant refried bean packages). Squeeze all the air out, cover the hole with a piece of tape. Place the food package into a quart size freezer ziplock bag. Close the ziplock bag with no air left in the ziplock bag. The tiny hole in the food package eliminates extra air, while the thick freezer ziplock bag helps keep the food fresh. DO NOT poke holes in jerky packages, unless you want rock-hard jerky.

- <u>Fill the mail drop box completely</u>. If there is extra space, add something to fill the box so there is no dead air. Imagine your package at the bottom of the mail truck. If the package has dead air space inside, it could easily get crushed. Crushed boxes often split open.

  Make the filler count! A bag of Fritos or a box of cookies are both great fillers. The filler doesn't have to be food you will take on the trail; it could be town snacks.

- <u>Shipping olive oil</u>: Purchase a large container of olive oil and several 8-ounce bottles of water. Empty the water bottles, air dry them completely, fill with as much olive oil as you will need for each resupply distance. Double-bag each bottle inside two ziplock bags.

- Use ziplock bags to <u>protect any liquids from leakage</u>. This applies to olive oil, condiment packets (mustard, mayo, hot sauce, etc.), contact solution, shampoo.

- <u>Wrap all toiletry items in aluminum foil</u>. The foil prevents soap fragrance from permeating your food. This applies to soap, shampoo, conditioner, shaving cream, etc.

- Put a piece of paper inside each package with both the <u>destination and return addresses</u>. Why is this important? Sometimes the mailing label on the outside of the box gets damaged. If that happens, the shipping service (USPS, UPS, FedEx, etc.) will open the package in an attempt to find out who it belongs to. Help the shipping service get the package to you!

- <u>Examine the box structure</u>. Boxes usually have a seam on one edge which is glued together. NEVER trust that the seam will hold together. ALWAYS reinforce that seam with packing tape.

- <u>Examine the box closure</u>. Some boxes have an adhesive strip which is presumably used to close the box securely. NEVER assume the adhesive will do the job. ALWAYS reinforce that area with packing tape.

- If you are <u>reusing a box which has been shipped before</u>, completely remove or black out any old mailing addresses, labels, and shipping bar codes.

- <u>Assign a number to each package</u> (see "Resupply Pick Up List" on page 58). Write that number on the outside of each package. It doesn't have to be large. Just make it easy for your home resupply person to find "Box Number Five" when you call and ask for something to be added to that package.

- Write the <u>shipping and return addresses</u> on the outside of each package.

- Write your <u>last name in great big bold letters</u> on all sides of every package.

- <u>Make your packages unique</u>: spray paint, stickers, etc. This helps if a Post Office, business, or Trail Angel cannot find your package. You can say, "my package has giant Zebra stickers on every side."

- When using mailing labels, <u>always secure the label to the box with packing tape</u>. Label stickers can come off the box during shipping. Packing tape helps prevent that.

- <u>Do not tape your packages shut</u>. Leaving them open allows your home resupply person to easily add/subtract from your packages if necessary.

ADDRESSING TRAIL MAIL

The recipient's name must be the hiker's legal name, which is the name listed on the hiker's government issued ID. Hikers often take trail names (i.e. nicknames). Trail names become a badge of honor, and many hikers do not know each other's legal name. Trail names are fun, but they are not useful when picking up mail at the Post Office.

Let's say Jane Smith has the trail name "Tiny Toes." Jane's Mom ships her resupply package to:

Tiny Toes
General Delivery
Town, State Zip Code

Jane goes to the Post Office to pick up her resupply package. If the Post Office Clerk can even find the package addressed to Tiny Toes, the Clerk won't release it to Jane, because Jane's ID shows her name as Jane Smith, not Tiny Toes.

It would be fine to address it to: "Jane Smith, aka Tiny Toes." In fact, the Post Office in Tuolumne Meadows (Yosemite National Park) along the Pacific Crest Trail requests that hikers write both their legal name and trail name on their packages. This is because when there is a Search and Rescue , the search teams ask hikers if they have seen the missing hiker "Jane Smith." Most of Jane's hiker friends do not know her legal name, but they do know "Tiny Toes."

Address format for USPS General Delivery without street address:	Hiker's Legal Name Trail Hiker, ETA: MM/DD/YY General Delivery Town, State Zip Code

Address format for USPS General Delivery WITH street address:	Hiker's Legal Name Trail Hiker, ETA: MM/DD/YY General Delivery Post Office Street Address Town, State Zip Code

Address format for all mail to hotels, businesses, or Trail Angels:	Hiker's Legal Name Trail Hiker, ETA: MM/DD/YY c/o Business or Trail Angel's Name Complete Address Town, State Zip Code

At the bottom left corner of all mail:	Hold for Trail Hiker ETA: (date)

ALWAYS double-check to make sure you used the correct destination Zip Code.

Instead of "Trail Hiker," you could customize the address for your trail. For example:

Appalachian Trail:	"Hold for AT Hiker"
Long Trail:	"Hold for LT Hiker"
Arizona Trail:	"Hold for AZT Hiker"
Pacific Crest Trail:	"Hold for PCT Hiker"
Continental Divide Trail:	"Hold for CDT Hiker"
John Muir Trail:	"Hold for JMT Hiker"
Florida Trail:	"Hold for FT Hiker"

PARTNERS RECEIVING MAIL

Packages addressed to two or more hikers must include the name of each person who could pick up the package.

Let's say Jane Smith and Bob Johnson are hiking together. Jane hikes faster than Bob, so Jane usually gets to town first. Jane wants to pick up their USPS General Delivery package from the Post Office, go to the motel, and wait for Bob to arrive. In order for Jane to pick up the package, it must be addressed like this:

Jane Smith or Bob Johnson
General Delivery
Town, State Zip Code

Notice it is:	Jane Smith	*OR*	Bob Johnson
It is NOT:	Jane Smith	*AND*	Bob Johnson

If Jane encounters a Postal Clerk who is a stickler for the rules, and if the package was addressed to Jane AND Bob, the Postal Clerk might require both Jane and Bob to be present to receive the package. However, if the package is addressed to Jane OR Bob, the Postal Clerk can release the package to either person. The same idea applies to hikers with the same last name. Address the package to: Jane OR Bob Smith, not Jane AND Bob Smith.

Trail mail is usually shelved alphabetically by last name. When Jane presents her ID to the postal clerk and asks for her package, Jane should let the Postal Clerk know that the package could be under "Smith" or "Johnson."

RESUPPLY PICK UP LIST

Make a list of every place the hiker will resupply, showing not only places where the hiker will pick up a box but also places where the hiker will buy food. This list should be simple, yet contain necessary information for both the home resupply person and the hiker.

- The list contains all the information necessary for the <u>home resupply person</u> to easily ship packages to the hiker.

- The list contains information the <u>hiker</u> needs to know about the packages they will receive and places where the hiker will purchase food.

Sample Resupply Pick Up List

Pickup Location	Box #	*Shipping Method* Shipping Address	Days of Food	Fuel or Gear
Town A mile point 75 ETA: 5-1-21	1	*USPS Priority Mail* Hiker's Legal Name Trail Hiker, ETA: MM/DD/YY General Delivery Town A, State, Zip Code	4	No

- When the hiker arrives in Town A, he picks up a resupply package at the Post Office.
- This is Box #1, which was shipped using USPS Priority Mail.
- The package contains 4 days of food, which is enough to cover the 65 trail miles from Town A to Town B.
- Box #1 does not contain any fuel or gear.

Pickup Location	Box #	Shipping Address	Days of Food	Fuel or Gear
Town B mile point 140 ETA: 5-5-21	N/A	Buy food in town	3	N/A

- When the hiker arrives in Town B, he does not receive a resupply package. He goes to the supermarket in Town B.
- He buys 3 days of food, which is enough to cover the 55 trail miles from Town B to Town C.

Pickup Location	Box #	Shipping Address	Days of Food	Fuel or Gear
Town C mile point 195 ETA: 5-10-21	2	*USPS Priority Mail* Hiker's Legal Name Trail Hiker, ETA: MM/DD/YY General Delivery Street Address Town C, State, Zip Code	5	Maps

- When the hiker arrives in Town C, he picks up a resupply package at the Post Office.
- This is Box #2, which was shipped using USPS Priority Mail to a General Delivery address which requires the street address.
- The package contains 5 days of food, which is enough to cover the 85 trail miles from Town C to Town D.
- In addition to food, Box #2 also contains maps.

Sample Resupply Pick Up List

Pickup Location	Box #	Shipping Method Shipping Address	Days of Food	Fuel or Gear
Town D mile point 280 *ETA: 5-14-21*	**3**	*USPS Retail Ground* Hiker's Legal Name Trail Hiker, ETA: MM/DD/YY General Delivery Town D, State, Zip Code	4	Fuel

- When the hiker arrives in Town D, he picks up a resupply package at the Post Office.
- This is Box #3. Because it contains fuel, it was shipped Retail Ground instead of Priority Mail (see page 62). Retail Ground takes longer than Priority Mail, so the home resupply person had to get this box in the mail earlier than usual.
- The package contains 4 days of food, which is enough to cover the 80 trail miles from Town D to Town E.
- In addition to food, Box #3 also contains fuel.

Pickup Location	Box #	Shipping Method Shipping Address	Days of Food	Fuel or Gear
Town E mile point 360 *ETA: 5-18-21*	**4**	*UPS or FedEx* Hiker's Legal Name Trail Hiker, ETA: MM/DD/YY c/o Hotel Name Complete Address Town E, State, Zip Code	4	Shoes

- When the hiker arrives in Town E, he picks up a resupply package at the hotel.
- This is Box #4, which was shipped using either UPS or FedEx. The package contains 4 days of food, which is enough to get to the next town.
- In addition to food, this box also contains shoes.

Notice that Boxes 1 and 2 are both USPS General Delivery addresses. Box 1 does not contain a street address, but Box 2 does. That is because some USPS General Delivery addresses require street addresses, some should not have street addresses. Be sure to review the General Delivery information on page 74. If you are unsure if you should include the street address or not, call the DESTINATION Post Office.

Place a copy of the Resupply Pick Up List inside every resupply box. It is extremely helpful for the hiker to have this list so he is aware of his upcoming resupply plans. If a copy is placed in each box, the hiker does not need to hold on to the plan while he is hiking. Each time he receives a box, he can review the plan for the next few resupply locations, make mental note of the plan, then discard the printed page. It is also helpful to save the Resupply Pick Up List digitally on the hiker's phone.

GEAR LEFT AT HOME

You may have some gear and clothing which you might need later during your hike. You'll leave this gear/clothing with your home resupply person. When you need your lightweight long-sleeved Capilene zip-neck Patagonia shirt, you'll just call your resupply person and ask them to put that shirt in your next mail drop. But what if they don't know the difference between a Capilene shirt and a wind shirt?

Here's what you do: Place each piece of "I might need that sometime" gear in its own ziplock bag. With a black marker, and in big print, write numbers and gear descriptions on note cards. Write one number on each card: one through fifteen, or however many ziplock bags you've got filled with gear. Slide a numbered card into each ziplock bag. Make sure the number is easily seen through the ziplock bag.

Make a list of all your numbered bags and the contents. Leave the list with your home resupply person digitally and on paper. Save a copy on the hiker's phone. Then, when you need that lightweight long-sleeved Capilene zip-neck Patagonia shirt, look at your gear list. The shirt you want is in bag number 3. Call your resupply person and ask them to put bag number 3 in your next resupply package. All they have to do is look for the large black 3 written on the yellow card which is in the ziplock bag with the shirt. They put bag #3 in your next resupply package. No confusion.

SHIPPING FUEL

Can you ship canister fuel? Short answer is yes. However, shipping fuel is tricky. There are two main restrictions:

- The package must ship using <u>ground transportation</u> (not air mail), which means it cannot ship via USPS Priority Mail.

- The package must be <u>clearly marked</u> on the address side of the package with these words:

> Surface Mail Only
> Consumer Commodity ORM-D

There are other restrictions, and there is a quantity limit per package. The regulations are extensive and exhausting to interpret. Even the Postal Clerks do not always know the specifics on shipping fuel.

Triple-Crowners Ken and Marcia Powers (aka "Gottawalk") have meticulously researched the regulations for shipping fuel. For many years, thru-hikers have used Gottawalk's fuel information. If you ship canister fuel, be sure to familiarize yourself with the regulations: click the GEAR TALK tab at [www.triplecrownoutfitters.com].

BOUNCE BOX

A bounce box contains items you need occasionally but don't want to carry with you while you hike. You mail your bounce box to a trail town address (Post Office, motel, Trail Angel). Pick up the box, take things out of or put things into the box, then ship it ahead (bounce it) to yourself further up the trail. This may sound like a great idea, but managing a bounce box can be frustrating:

- You'll constantly modify your hike to be in town during Post Office hours.

- If you ship your bounce box to a location which does not have outgoing mail, you've got a problem.

- You'll spend a fortune on postage.

CARE PACKAGES

Your family and friends may want to send you packages and letters on the trail. Provide them with a list of your mail drop locations along with this information:

- I have to ask for all my mail, so <u>don't send "surprise" packages</u>. Text or email me to let me know you sent a care package (and where it was sent).

- The mail drop list <u>ETA dates are estimates</u>. I may be there a week early or late.

- Be sure to use the proper carrier (USPS, UPS, or FedEx). <u>USPS packages should always ship using USPS Priority Mail</u>. Never use USPS Retail Ground (the only exception is a package containing fuel).

- <u>Letters can be sent USPS First Class</u>.

- <u>Address mail exactly as shown</u> on my mail drop list.

- <u>Write on every package/letter</u>: "Hold for Trail Hiker. ETA: MM/DD/YY"

SHIPPING PACKAGES

WHERE DO HIKERS RECEIVE MAIL?

Hikers receive mail at trail town Post Offices, businesses, motels, or Trail Angel homes. There is no fee to pick up USPS General Delivery at a Post Office. Some businesses and Trail Angels charge a fee to securely hold hiker packages.

Pay close attention to the information contained in the guidebook for your trail. Guidebooks usually indicate if an address accepts all mail carriers or if it is "USPS only," "UPS only," "UPS or FedEx only." Be absolutely sure you use the proper shipping service for the destination address.

Post Office

USPS General Delivery is the safest, most secure way to receive trail mail. Pick up USPS General Delivery at the trail town Post Office. Postal Clerks will release mail only to the addressee, who must show a government issued ID (Driver's License, Passport, State Identification Card, etc.).

Be sure to use USPS General Delivery if your package contains important items such as a passport. Do NOT send important items to a business, motel, or Trail Angel address.

Pros: Mail is secure. The only person who can pick up
          USPS General Delivery mail is the addressee.

Cons: Post Offices are always closed on federal
          holidays and Sundays, often closed on
          Saturdays, and sometimes have very limited
          hours Monday through Friday. The hiker must
          be mindful of Post Office hours to avoid waiting
          around in town for the Post Office to open.
          Waiting in town gets expensive (lodging and
          food costs).

Businesses

Many motels, outfitters, stores, and other businesses
accept hiker packages.

Pros: Usually open every day, either 24 hours a day or
          with long business hours.

Cons: Often there is a package fee, ranging from $5 to
          $50.

          Mail is not always secure. Hikers often are
          directed to the area where all hiker packages are
          stored. A hiker could easily take any package.

Trail Angels

Trail Angels are local residents who assist hikers with a variety of tasks: rides, package holding, computer use, meals, lodging. Trail Angels often accept hiker packages.

Pros: Hikers usually can pick up mail any time, any day of the week.

Cons: Sometimes there is a package fee, ranging from $5 to $50.

Mail is not always secure. Hikers often are directed to the area where all hiker packages are stored. A hiker could easily take any package.

UPS and FEDEX

Some businesses and Trail Angels are located in areas which do not have street delivery of USPS mail. Fortunately, UPS and FedEx typically deliver to these locations. Trail guidebooks usually note these as "UPS or FedEx only" addresses.

Compared to USPS Priority Mail, UPS and FedEx packages often cost more to ship, are delivered faster, and have better tracking information.

Shipments using USPS to a "UPS or FedEx only" address

When a package is mailed using USPS to a "UPS or FedEx only" address, it is possible that the clerk at the shipping Post Office will accept the package. The package could travel all the way to the destination town listed on the shipping address. At that point, the USPS will realize that there is not street delivery in that town, the package will be rejected and (hopefully) returned to sender. Bottom line: the hiker will not receive the package.

Shipments using UPS or FedEx to a "USPS only" address

Retailers such as Amazon and REI are notorious for using UPS or FedEx on a General Delivery address. A General Delivery address is a "USPS only" address. If your package is shipped using UPS or FedEx to a General Delivery address, there are two possible outcomes when UPS or FedEx attempt to deliver the package to the destination Post Office:

(1) The Post Office will reject the package. UPS/FedEx will probably return to sender. Bottom line: the hiker will not receive the package.

(2) The Post Office will accept the package. When the hiker picks up the package from the Post Office, the hiker will be charged USPS postage on top of UPS/FedEx postage fees which were

already paid. Bottom line: the hiker will receive the package, but will have to pay USPS postage.

HYBRID SHIPPING SYSTEMS

FedEx SmartPost and UPS SurePost are hybrid shipping systems where the package starts out in the hands of FedEx or UPS. When the package gets near the destination, it is turned over to the USPS. The USPS completes the delivery. This is often a nightmare in small trail towns, especially towns which do not have street delivery of USPS mail. FedEx/UPS will tell you that your package will ship with no problems; in reality you may never get it. ALWAYS ask FedEx/UPS if they are using only their delivery, or if it is a hybrid program involving the USPS.

This is a HUGE problem for hikers who order from large companies such as Amazon, Walmart, and REI. No matter what you tell the customer service representative regarding shipping options, the shipping personnel will always use the cheapest shipping available. That is often a hybrid shipping system.

USPS PRIORITY MAIL

USPS Priority Mail is supposed to take 2-3 business days to arrive. Due to the rural locations of many trail towns, allow 1-2 extra days travel time.

When shipping USPS, always use Priority Mail (one exception: packages containing fuel, which must ship ground, see page 62). If you use USPS First Class or Retail Ground, you could easily lose some of your packages. Also, don't believe the Post Office employees when they tell you they can have a Retail Ground package to your destination a week to 10 days from the date you mail it. That's not true. It won't make it. You must use Priority Mail.

If you send a USPS General Delivery package via Priority Mail, *AND* then decide you don't need it at that trail town, *AND* if you do not open the package or take it away from the Post Office counter, you *MIGHT* be allowed to bounce it ahead to your next trail town without paying any more postage. This used to be a common practice. However, per phone calls to many Post Offices, it is now against regulations to bounce boxes ahead for free, although some trail town Post Offices will still bounce packages for hikers.

It makes sense that bouncing a box for free would be against regulations:

- ► Hiker paid for postage from Town A to Town B.
- ► USPS delivered the package to Town B.
- ► The transaction is complete.
- ► If you want the package sent to Town C, that is a brand new transaction and requires proper postage from Town B to Town C.

Priority Mail Flat Rate

Priority Mail Flat Rate boxes cost the same to ship regardless of weight or destination. Medium and Large Flat Rate Boxes are commonly used for hiker resupply packages. You must use the boxes provided by the USPS. The boxes are free; you simply pay the postage. Boxes are available at [www.usps.com] or any Post Office.

Priority Mail Regional Rate

This is a quasi-flat rate service. Rate varies based upon distance traveled. Regional Rate boxes are cheaper for shorter shipping distances, Flat Rate boxes are cheaper for longer distances.

Regional Box A: Pay Priority Mail rate for ~ 2 pounds, can ship up to 15 pounds

Regional Box B: Pay Priority Mail rate for ~ 4 pounds, can ship up to 20 pounds

Regional Rate boxes are not available at Post Offices; they must be ordered from [www.usps.com]. Boxes usually take about two weeks to arrive. Boxes come side-loading or top-loading. You want the top-loading boxes: A1 or B1.

Here is how Regional Rate shipping works:

- Sign up for a USPS Click-N-Ship account (see page 80).

- Order Boxes A1 and B1 from the USPS website.

- Fill your boxes.

- Weigh your boxes.

- Use your Click-N-Ship account to create and print shipping labels with postage (see page 80).

- Drop your boxes off at the Post Office.

You are not required to use Click-N-Ship when shipping Regional Rate boxes. You can also ship Regional Rate boxes in person at the Post Office. However, many Postal Clerks are not familiar with Regional Rate boxes. They might charge you regular Priority Mail rates. Tell the Clerk it is a Regional Rate box, and ask them to scan the bar code on the box. Once they scan the bar code, the Regional Rate postage will appear on their system. There is a service fee to ship using Regional Rate boxes in person at the Post Office (in 2021, service fee is $2.30).

Priority Mail Boxes	Dimensions (inches)					cu in
Medium Flat 1	11.25	x	8.75	x	6	590
Medium Flat 2	12	x	3.5	x	14 1/8	593
Large Flat (GBFRB)	11 7/8	x	3.25	x	24 1/16	928
Large Flat (LARGEFRB)	12.25	x	12.25	x	6	900
Regional A1	10 1/8	x	7 1/8	x	5	360
Regional A2	11 1/16	x	2.5	x	13 1/16	361
Regional B1	12.25	x	10.5	x	5.5	707
Regional B2	14.5	x	3	x	16.25	706

Comparison: Priority Mail cost from San Diego to these towns	Reg A	Reg B	Med Flat	Lg Flat
Capacity (cu in):	360	707	590	900-928
Idyllwild CA	$7.83	$8.23	$15.50	$21.90
Etna CA	$8.34	$9.56	$15.50	$21.90
Skykomish WA	$10.89	$17.50	$15.50	$21.90
Lordsburg NM	$9.01	$12.36	$15.50	$21.90
Encampment WY	$9.01	$12.36	$15.50	$21.90
East Glacier MT	$10.89	$17.50	$15.50	$21.90
Franklin NC	$12.64	$22.90	$15.50	$21.90
Duncannon PA	$12.64	$22.90	$15.50	$21.90
Monson ME	$12.64	$22.90	$15.50	$21.90

Priority Mail Rates effective January 24, 2021					
Box Style	Box dimensions			Weight Limit	Cost
	L	W	H		
Flat Rate Medium	11"	8.5"	5.5"	no limit	$15.50
Flat Rate Large	12"	12"	5.5"	no limit	$21.90
Regional Box A1	10"	7"	4.75"	15 pounds	$7.83 and up
Regional Box B1	12"	10.25"	5"	20 pounds	$8.23 and up

USPS GENERAL DELIVERY

[https://faq.usps.com/s/article/What-is-General-Delivery]

Per the USPS website: "General Delivery is a mail service for those without a permanent address, often used as a temporary mailing address." Trail town Post Offices have accepted hiker USPS General Delivery for many, many years.

If there is more than one Post Office in a town, usually only the Main Post Office accepts USPS General Delivery mail.

You might think that all Post Offices follow the same General Delivery procedures. Unfortunately, this is not the case. If you call two different Post Offices, you could get different answers to the same questions. If you call the same Post Office twice, you could get different answers to the same questions. For example:

(1) <u>Inconsistency #1</u>: Some Postmasters will tell you that you MUST include the <u>physical street address of the Post Office</u> when addressing General Delivery mail.

<u>Inconsistency #2</u>: Some Postmasters will tell you the physical street address is not necessary, but you can include it if you want to.

<u>Inconsistency #3</u>: Some Postmasters in towns which do not have street delivery of mail will tell you that if you include the physical street address for their specific Post Office on a General Delivery address, the package will automatically be returned to sender.

<u>Inconsistency #4</u>: The USPS website states General Delivery should be addressed like this:

> NAME
> GENERAL DELIVERY
> CITY STATE ZIP

And it gets more confusing. You may have a package sent General Delivery to a town where a physical street address will result in the package being returned to sender. You *know* you cannot include the physical street address. But, the Clerk at the Post Office where you are mailing the package from could tell you the street address is required on the General Delivery address.

(2) <u>Post Office policy is that General Delivery is held for no more than 30 days</u>; if it is not picked up in 30 days, it will be returned to sender. Most trail Post Offices will hold hiker mail much longer than 30 days, because the Postmasters have been working with hikers for many years and they know that hikers eventually show up. However, some Postmasters are sticklers for the rules, and will not bend them for anyone.

(3) <u>Post Office policy is that any mail with a tracking number must be picked up within 15 days of arrival</u>; if it is not picked up in 15 days, it will be returned to sender.

As a favor to hikers, if a package has reached 15 days, some Postmasters will scan the tracking numbers as "delivered." They will keep the package at the Post Office until the hiker pick it up. The problem with this is that you could look online to see the status of your package, it shows as "delivered," you KNOW you have not picked it up, you panic thinking someone else has your package. In reality, the Postmaster was simply doing you a favor. It's a Catch-22.

(4) <u>What happens to a General Delivery package with a tracking number</u>?

- Per (2) above, General Delivery is supposed to be held for 30 days, then returned to sender.

- Per (3) above, items with tracking numbers are supposed to be held for 15 days, then returned to sender.

- ALL packages have tracking numbers (including General Delivery).

So . . . . . . will the Post Office return your General Delivery package after 15 days, after 30 days, or scan it as delivered and hold it until you arrive? Different Post Offices handle this differently. The only way to know for sure is to call the destination Post Office directly (the Post Office where the hiker will receive the package). Do not call the general USPS phone number, do not call the Post Office where you mailed the package from. Always err on the conservative side, and assume your hiker mail will only be held for 15 days.

(5) <u>Post Office policy is that General Delivery mail MUST have the words "General Delivery" in the address</u>. Without the words "General Delivery," packages are supposed to be rejected. As a favor to

hikers, some trail town Postmasters will hold incorrectly addressed hiker mail, because the Postmasters recognize hiker mail when they see it.

(6) General Delivery is for USPS mail only.
      General Delivery is for USPS mail only.
      General Delivery is for USPS mail only.

Mail shipped by UPS or FedEx to a General Delivery address which includes the street address of the Post Office might be accepted by the destination Post Office or it might be rejected. If it is accepted, the Post Office will hold it using their General Delivery Policy. However, when the hiker picks up the package, he will be required to pay USPS postage. Yes, he already paid UPS/FedEx postage, but now the package is in the hands of the USPS, so now he must pay USPS postage.

This is all very confusing. Fortunately, Postmasters genuinely want customers to receive their mail. Postmasters in trail towns are especially helpful. If you have any questions regarding your shipments, simply call the destination Post Office.

Here's an example: Let's say your home resupply person mailed a USPS General Delivery package to you on July 1. The package has a tracking number. It arrives at the destination Post Office on July 5. Because it has a tracking number, you must pick it up by July 20 (must be picked up within 15 days of arrival at the Post Office). But maybe you got delayed and you won't arrive in town until July 25. Don't panic. Call the destination Post Office before July 20, be polite and kind, ask them to hold your package until you arrive. Chances are very good that they will keep it for you. In fact, the USPS General Delivery website (above) states, "General Delivery mail may be held for longer periods if requested by sender or addressee and approved by postmaster."

SIGNATURE MAIL SERVICES

If the hiker's package is shipped using any method other than USPS General Delivery, make sure that the hiker does NOT have to sign for it.

For example: The hiker's package is shipped with signature confirmation to a business or Trail Angel. It's possible that the shipping service will not leave the package at the business or home if the addressee (the hiker) is not there to sign for it. Instead, depending upon which shipping service was used, the package will be held at the Post Office, UPS Customer Service Center, or FedEx Customer Service Center. Those locations could be several miles away in another town.

If the package is shipped USPS General Delivery, signature confirmation is fine because General Delivery mail stays in the possession of the USPS at the Post Office until the hiker picks it up.

USPS TEXT or EMAIL TRACKING

You can be notified of the status of your USPS package. Go to [www.usps.com], enter your tracking number, in the "Text & Email Updates" section choose "all below updates". Enter either your cell phone number or your email address. You will get a text or email every time the package status changes.

USPS CLICK-N-SHIP

Using USPS Click-N-Ship, consumers weigh their packages at home, log on to the USPS website, then print a postage-paid mailing label. It's fast, easy, and you don't have to stand in line at the Post Office.

The hiker should make Click-N-Ship easy for the home resupply person. While planning his hike, the hiker should set up the Click-N-Ship account, enter all the shipping addresses, set up all the email/text notifications, and put a credit card on file. If everything is set up properly, the home resupply person can easily print postage-paid labels and get packages out to the hiker very quickly. Here's how it works:

Create a Click-N-Ship Account

- Go to [www.usps.com].

- Hover over "Send," then click "Click-N-Ship."

- Follow the instructions to set up your account.

- Set the return address as the home resupply person's address.

- Set the email address as the hiker's email address.

- After setting up your account, every time you sign in you will be directed to the shipping page, which has five tabs:

  > Create Label
  > Preferences
  > Shipping History
  > Address Book
  > Shipping Cart

Set up Shipping Preferences

- Go into the Preferences tab.

- Under "Shipment Notifications," enter the home resupply person's email address and/or phone number (texts).

- Under "Notify Recipient of Shipping," check the box "Automatically notify recipient of shipping."

- Under "Return Address," enter the home resupply person's address.

Create Your Address Book

- Go into the Address Book tab.

- Add each resupply location as a contact, using the examples shown in the tables below.

- There are three types of shipping locations. The tables below give instructions for how to create Click-N-Ship labels for each location type:

(1) Shipments to stores, motels, Trail Angels.

(2) Shipments to a USPS General Delivery Post Office address WITHOUT a physical street address.

(3) Shipments to a USPS General Delivery Post Office address WITH a physical street address.

Click-N-Ship Address Example #1: Shipments to stores, motels, Trail Angels	
Scenario:	Ship a package to a Pacific Crest Trail (PCT) hiker. Hiker picks up package at a motel.
Click-N-Ship field	Enter this information
First Name	Jackie McDonnell, (note the comma after my last name)
Last Name	PCT Hiker, ETA: 04-15-21
Check box	"This address is a business" Check this box. After checking that box, the "Company" field is revealed.
Company	Use the "Company" field for the store name, hotel name, or Trail Angel's name. Begin the "Company" field with "c/o".

c/o Laguna Mountain Lodge |

Click-N-Ship Address Example #1:
Shipments to stores, motels, Trail Angels

Scenario: Ship a package to a Pacific Crest Trail (PCT) hiker. Hiker picks up package at a motel.

Click-N-Ship field	Enter this information
Nickname	The "Nickname" field is not required, but using nicknames helps to sort your address book. Nicknames should relate to the addresses. For example, you could use "Mount Laguna General Delivery" and "Mount Laguna Store" as nicknames. Nicknames do not appear on the label, but do appear in the address list – making it easier to find addresses at a glance.
Address Type	From drop-down menu, choose "Other"
Address	PO Box 146
City	Mount Laguna
State	CA
Zip Code	91948
Phone Number	This is supposed to be the phone number of the recipient. Some hikers put the store, motel, or Trail Angel's phone number; other hikers put the hiker's phone number.

Click-N-Ship Address Example #1:
Shipments to stores, motels, Trail Angels

Scenario:	Ship a package to a Pacific Crest Trail (PCT) hiker. Hiker picks up package at a motel.

Click-N-Ship field	Enter this information
Email Address	Enter the home resupply person's email address. The USPS will send tracking information to this email address. The hiker will get tracking via email because the hiker's email address was already entered when the account was set up.
Save Contact	Click the blue button "Save Contact"

The resulting Click-N-Ship address label will look like this:

Jackie McDonnell, PCT Hiker, ETA: 04-15-21
c/o Laguna Mountain Lodge
PO Box 146
Mount Laguna, CA 91948

Click-N-Ship Address Example #2:
Shipments to General Delivery Post Office address WITHOUT a physical street address

Scenario: Ship a package to a Pacific Crest Trail (PCT) hiker. Hiker picks up package at the Mount Laguna CA Post Office.

Click-N-Ship field	Enter this information
First Name	Jackie McDonnell, (note the comma after my last name)
Last Name	PCT Hiker, ETA: 04-15-21
Check box	"This address is a business" Do not check this box.
Nickname	The "Nickname" field is not required, but using nicknames helps to sort your address book. Nicknames should relate to the addresses. For example, you could use "Mount Laguna General Delivery" and "Mount Laguna Store" as nicknames. Nicknames do not appear on the label, but do appear in the address list – making it easier to find addresses at a glance.
Address Type	From drop-down menu, choose "Other"
Address	General Delivery (note it is *NOT* c/o General Delivery)
City	Mount Laguna

Click-N-Ship Address Example #2: Shipments to General Delivery Post Office address WITHOUT a physical street address

Scenario:	Ship a package to a Pacific Crest Trail (PCT) hiker. Hiker picks up package at the Mount Laguna CA Post Office.

Click-N-Ship field	Enter this information
State	CA
Zip Code	91948
Phone Number	This is supposed to be the phone number of the recipient. Some hikers put the Post Office phone number; other hikers put the hiker's phone number.
Email Address	Enter the home resupply person's email address. The USPS will send tracking information to this email address. The hiker will get tracking via email because the hiker's email address was already entered when the account was set up.
Save Contact	Click the blue button "Save Contact"

The resulting Click-N-Ship address label will look like this:

Jackie McDonnell, PCT Hiker, ETA: 04-15-21
General Delivery
Mount Laguna, CA 91948

Click-N-Ship Address Example #3: Shipments to General Delivery Post Office address WITH a physical street address

Scenario:	**Ship a package to a Pacific Crest Trail (PCT) hiker. Hiker picks up package at the Tehachapi CA Post Office.**

Click-N-Ship field	Type in this information
First Name	Jackie McDonnell, (note the comma after my last name)
Last Name	PCT Hiker, ETA: 04-15-21
Check box	"This address is a business" Check this box. After checking that box, the "Company" field is revealed.
Company	General Delivery (note it is *NOT* c/o General Delivery)
Nickname	The "Nickname" field is not required, but using nicknames helps to sort your address book. Nicknames should relate to the addresses. For example, you could use "Tehachapi General Delivery" and "Tehachapi Motel" as nicknames. Nicknames do not appear on the label, but do appear in the address list – making it easier to find addresses at a glance.
Address Type	From drop-down menu, choose "Other"

Click-N-Ship Address Example #3: Shipments to General Delivery Post Office address WITH a physical street address	
Address	1085 Voyager Drive
City	Tehachapi
State	CA
Zip Code	93581
Phone Number	This is supposed to be the phone number of the recipient. Some hikers put the Post Office phone number; other hikers put the hiker's phone number.
Email Address	Enter the home resupply person's email address. The USPS will send tracking information to this email address. The hiker will get tracking via email because the hiker's email address was already entered when the account was set up.
Save Contact	Click the blue button "Save Contact"

The resulting Click-N-Ship address label will look like this:

Jackie McDonnell, PCT Hiker, ETA: 04-15-21
General Delivery
1085 Voyager Drive
Tehachapi, CA 93581

Create a Label

Go to www. usps.com
Hover over "Send"
Click "Click-N-Ship"
Click on the tab "Create a Label"

- <u>Step 1: Return Address</u>: Where are you sending from?

   Return Address
   > The default return address is the address on
   > your Click-N-Ship account. You already set this
   > up as the home resupply person's address (see
   > page 81).

   More Actions
   > Always check "Send me tracking notifications."
   > This automatically sends tracking to the email
   > address or cell phone number on your Click-N-
   > Ship account. You already set this up as the
   > hiker's email or cell number (see page 81).

   Send me notifications for
   > Click the radio button for "All Updates."

   Ship from another ZIP Code
   > Check this box only if appropriate.

- Step 2: Delivery Address: Where are you sending to?

  Click "Use Address Book"

  Choose the appropriate address. The hiker already
      entered all his trail town addresses (see page 82).

  Scroll down.   Under "More Actions," check "Send
      recipient an email notification."   The hiker
      (recipient) is already getting a notification (see
      "Step 1, More Actions" above). You could enter
      the home resupply person's email here.

- Step 3: Shipping Date

  Choose a date as far out as 3 days from today.

- Step 4: Package Details

  This is where it gets tricky.

  Regional Rate boxes:
      DO NOT choose "Ship Flat Rate."
      Instead, choose "Ship by Package Weight."
      Then enter the weight.

  Flat Rate boxes:
      Choose "Ship Flat Rate."

Any other type of box:
>   Choose "Ship by Package Weight."
>   Then enter the weight.
>   Check this option only if applicable:
>>   This package has a dimension measuring
>>   over 12"

Package Value: Whatever you want.
>   Priority Mail automatically has $50 insurance.

- ## Step 5: Service Type

    Priority Mail is recommended.
    Click the blue box "Select Service and Packaging"

    IMPORTANT: If you chose "I am Shipping Flat Rate"
    under "Step 4: Package Details" above, you will NOT
    see Regional Rate box options on this table.

    Click the proper package size, then scroll down.

- ## Insurance and Extra Services

    Signature confirmation is not recommended for hiker
    mail sent to Trail Angels or businesses. Sometimes
    shipping services will not leave packages with signature
    confirmation unless the addressee is present to sign for
    the package. The hiker will usually not be at the
    location when the package arrives. Signature

confirmation is fine for USPS General Delivery, because General Delivery mail stays in the possession of the USPS until the hiker arrives at the Post Office to pick it up.

- <u>Click Add to Cart</u>

  After adding to cart, you can edit, delete, create another label, or check out.

- <u>Billing Information</u>

  The hiker can leave a credit card on file, then the home resupply person can easily purchase the postage.

- <u>Click Pay and Print</u>

  This automatically charges your card.

- <u>Print Labels or Save as PDF</u>

  Save it as PDF. This allows you to always have a copy of the label (to reprint or find the tracking number). The home resupply person can email the PDF label to the hiker.

START PACKING!

Hopefully, this book has provided a good understanding of nutritional trail food choices, mail drop logistics, and package shipping scenarios.

Keep in mind that in order for a mail drop program to work smoothly, the home resupply person and the hiker must work well together. The hiker must give the home resupply person ample notice to ship the packages; the home resupply person must understand that if the hiker needs the package in the mail no later than June 27, shipping it on June 28 is too late.

Careful pre-hike mail drop planning will alleviate mental stress while on trail.

If, after reading this book, you have any questions about mail drops, feel free to shoot us an email: yogisbooks@gmail.com

Enjoy your hike!